For paper back book copies of Funeral For Pennies On A
Dollar send payment to: G.T.M. 731 Portland, ME. 04104.
You can find this book on www.gtmministries.org.
Copyright Pending

Dedication

This book is dedicated with much thanks and gratitude to Father God for his faithful love and guidance through this extremely trying time.

Next to my loving and dear earthly father Harland G. Delaney that passed away November 23 rd. 2009. He made many people happy with his amazing sense of humor and caring ways. He was a man of faith.

I know he would not have wanted us to be burdened financially and he would be blessed and delighted to know that his and our experience has helped others.

Much love and appreciation to my Aunt Rose for her many visits to see and care for my father when he was ill. Much love to

Aunt Kay for her many years of caring and prayers for Dad.

Love to Uncle George, Aunt Marcia and the family for their visit having traveled such a distance from New Hampshire. Many thanks for their care, prayers, love and concern.

Many thanks to my brothers Tony Fator and Gil Delaney. Their kind generosity, loving support and caring made this possible. Tony has risen up to be present to serve and care when family has needed comfort and encouragement most. We are proud of him since he has a very good heart.

Much love and appreciation to my dear husband Reverend Ralph Knight for his love, great ideas, support and prayers.

And love to my online face book family that gave so much support.

Funeral For Pennies On A Dollar

Introduction

In 2009 we suddenly found ourselves responsible for my father's funeral and expenses. I began to journal.

In this economy every penny matters. This book is a journal of steps that saved us thousands of dollars. God was so good to provide the wisdom we needed as he led us through, so we give Him all the credit and glory. I know there are many others that will face the same financial decisions and pray this will be of help to many.

Funeral For Pennies On The Dollar provides insight and options that can bring you major savings. The large bill that we could have been paying on for years never came. It did not happen since we learned how to save thousands in only a few simple steps and you can learn how too. You can learn how to avoid the tidal wave of expense that comes with funerals. Every family should read this and become informed on how to face those final hours with peace of mind.

Table of Contents

Funeral For Pennies On A Dollar

The doctor on the other end of the phone was serious and emotional. She said she had been trying to reach us all day and said that your Dad is not well. You need to be aware of the situation Laurie, his heart stopped and we have been working on him through out the afternoon! We have been trying frantically to bring him back to life!! His vitals have drop incredibly low.

Dad was way overweight for years and had suffered a heart attack a couple of years back while also living with diabetes. We knew he had health issues and expected that he may take a sudden and drastic downturn, and he did.

It was surreal and hard to believe that we were now entering the final days. The many wonderful moments looking into my father's gentle brown eyes, seeing his big smile and hearing him say I love you Laurie and I'm proud of you would soon come to an end. His heart beat with child like innocence that was full of wonder, joy and unconditional love for people and nature. He had a very funny and rare sense of humor. I told him often that he should have had his own TV show.

It seemed only yesterday that I was standing beside him in the car as a small child with my arms wrapped tightly around him as we drove the many miles to see friends and family.

Dad loved me with an unconditional love and I knew it. I would always be his little girl no matter the challenges we had to face together in life. Even in this critical hour I still felt the strong support and love he had poured out on me over the years rise up to meet this challenge. He told me shortly before this final turn of events that I was to be strong for him and with God's help I was.

I had just spoken with Dad the day before and his voice was weak. I could tell he was having trouble breathing but was not too concerned since he had been on oxygen for sometime and seemed to be doing well.

The phone calls continued to come. The doctor asked us just what our plans were if he should pass away. My husband and I just looked at each other. We were clueless and suddenly realized that we were solely responsible for funeral arrangements since Dad had canceled his burial insurance only a matter of months before. He could not afford the money for his medications, food and rent so he felt he had to do away with the insurance coverage. We were close financially too so we had no way to help.

Now understanding his acute condition we were not aware of the financial tidal wave that was suddenly on the way and envisioned the months or even years that we would be making payments from funeral home services. With my husband newly retired and on a small pension, me unemployed due to health issues and the slowing economy, who knows if we could even begin to pay it off!!! My husband is also a number of years older and will be in his 70s this year, so to have the financial pressure of possibly another funeral in the near future was a major concern. I suddenly had to be informed. I had to figure out a way to provide an affordable funeral for my father. Something that would provide the dignity due him but also that would financially bless us and our family who would have to deal with the bills after the funeral and burial was completed.

A Blessed Legacy

Hard to believe my father's brief time on life's stage would soon be coming come to an end. He called himself the entertainer and that he was.

Dad's sense of humor came natural for his song writing and guitar playing. His amazing gift of music and melodies that he played were a rare treat as he played the song Autumn Leaves with full rich tones that swept your senses into the colorful autumn season. Tunes that few accomplished musicians could master.

Dad's wonderful legacy of music would be passed onto me and my brother Gil but his talent will be forever missed.

The most important legacy was passing down faith in God. He loved God and was sure to have us in church faithfully. His music ministry was powerful as he directed many through song to the saving knowledge of Jesus Christ.

The roller coaster health reports continued to come in so I immediately began contacting family for financial help.

I had the medical staff take measurements of Dad while he was sleeping. My father weighed in at just over 400 lbs. his measurements were 6 ft. x 42 wide by 22 inches high. The actual coffin size measured out at 6'7 x 45 x 25 high. So everything had to be double the size. I had to plan a funeral for two basically.

The following information is a true story and has not been easy for me to journal. It is shared primarily to help those that are going through financial struggles and will be dealing with the reality of having to provide a proper funeral for family members on basically a shoe string budget.

After hearing the news of my father's critical condition, I found myself rising above the emotional sadness and stress of the moment to understanding the responsibility I had to take on during my father's final days. I became aware of what his casket alone would cost, the burial plot to the stone, and on and on. I began to see the final outcome on paper and learned that a major expense was on the way....and major miracles...

The following simple steps can apply in just about every state. A few regulations may vary in some states and so it is good to do research online and call your cemetery caretaker through your local town office and find out about requirements that may apply as you make funeral preparations. Each county has its own requirements. Keep in mind that they are not state law.

Has a family member lost their burial insurance coverage? Have they suddenly come down with a serious illness and may not have much time to live? Are you in financial stress of your own and also other members of your family are not able to help since they are financially up against it too? I was there and here is my step by step method to secure a funeral at a fraction of the cost, and with only a few simple steps.

Did you know that you do not have to go through a funeral home and absorb their outrageous markups? Some as high as 700%? Do you know that there is no law that requires your loved one to be embalmed? Do you know that Maine state law does not require a burial vault or grave liner? (A container that holds or incases the casket.)

In this book you will learn secrets to cut corners big time on funeral cost. These steps can be implemented much quicker for you since I have applied and walked out the simple steps in this booklet. I have learned first hand through the loss of family just what you will need to do to see a memorable family held funeral come together successfully and quickly. The savings will be amazing.

Memories of Father

Dad had a real sense of humor and loved driving and site seeing. He loved sea food too. He said to be sure to put stripped fish in his casket and also a steering wheel since he would love having stripped fish to snack on as he drove off into eternity. I did neither of the two; however I do plan to put stripped fish on his grave someday soon. Stripped fish is fish that is cut into thin strips that has been dried on lines in the sun. A treat that only down east fisherman and their families can understand and enjoy. My father's dad was a fisherman so my dad grew to love stripped fish, scallops, steamed clams and lobsters dipped in butter.

Dad would laugh and carry on as he wanted me to promise that I would follow through with his wishes and be sure to put stripped fish in his casket!

Times have changed

It has only been in the last 70 years that we have changed the traditional family burial to one that has been put in the hands of our local funeral home. It used to be that a relative would be on display in a casket in the parlor for a few days for the family to view and then was buried in the family cemetery. It used to be common practice that the family would take the responsibility to plan and care for their loved ones burial. Today we send those that pass away to funeral homes and let them take care of the arrangements costing those that are still living years of unnecessary funeral bills and cost to cover. If they do not have burial insurance there will be great expense that the family is left to pay out of pocket. If members of the family pitch in then that is good, but most can only afford $100.00 dollars or so each. The average funeral cost as much as $7,000.00 and greater leaving someone with a hefty bill to pay.

You can save thousands in only a few simple steps. We need substantial cost effective savings tips in this economy. For those of us that find that our family member is not covered with burial insurance or would like to avoid the monthly cost of paying on burial insurance then this is the book to read. Also if you have an ill family member and want to give them a proper burial but need to save money then this is for you.

Begin making plans now...

You need to prepare and become educated before the difficult season arrives. This book is a major step in the right direction. If these steps are implemented before the difficult days occur you will be well prepared for the final hours. You can also apply this information within days like I did but it is suggested to have things in place a few months before hand.

Cremation Vs. Traditional Burial

A friend lost family members and had them cremated. It cost my friend $4,000 for each person. Personally I come from a traditional Christian back ground and so my husband and I desire to bury family with Christian burials.

Please understand that these are not comments against cremation but views to help you better understand Christian burial and why you should do some research before you choose cremation. A Christian burial can be done for a fraction of the cost. Either way it is a choice you will have to live with and generations will most likely repeat.

Abraham is the father of the Christian faith. He was called by God to leave his home land and go to a strange new land in order to establish the nation of Israel, God's chosen people. The following is taken from the Bible. These are some of the Christian burial practices that have influenced the church to this day.

The death of Abraham, his wife Sarah and Isaac in the book of Genesis 25: 9, 10.

And his son Isaac and Ishmael <u>buried him</u> in the grave of Machpelah, in the field of Ephron the son of Zohar the Hittite which is before Mamre;

The field which Abraham purchased of the sons of Heth: Genisis 23: 3-16 There was Abraham buried, and Sarah his wife.

Genesis 49

29 And he charged them, and said unto them, I am to be gathered unto my people: <u>bury me</u> with my fathers in the cave that is in the field of Ephron the Hittite.

30 In the cave that is in the field of Machpelah which is before Mamre, in the Land of Canaan, *which Abraham bought with the field of Ephron the Hittite for a possession of a <u>burying place.</u>*

31There <u>they buried Abraham</u> <u>and</u> <u>Sarah his wife;</u> <u>there they buried Isaac</u> and Rebekah his wife; and there I <u>buried Leah</u>.

So you can see the no one was burned but buried in complete body form.

Then the second ruler to the throne of Egypt, Abraham's descendent Jacob's son Joseph and his <u>body carried up</u> during the Exodus from Egypt.

Jesus Christ the Son of God upon his death was not burned <u>but buried in the tomb</u> of a wealthy man. He was the Son of God and rose the third day. Also Christians after the death and resurrection of Christ were buried in catacombs.

So according to Christian burial we are to keep our bodies as they are in hope of the return of the Lord. Being kept whole and not burned.

Cremation is no new idea....

For many centuries it was the almost universal custom of Ayran peoples – Indians, Greeks, Romans, Slavs, Teutons, etc. to burn their dead. The practice of cremation was suppressed gradually in favor of Christian burial, where Christianity took root. The teaching of the truth of the resurrection of the body, and the accountability to God resulting their from, brought about this change. Cremation is still practiced today. Just do a Google search on the subject and you can read the different views. Where there are typhoons and tsunamis there are usually mass deaths that occur and the only way to take care of the dead is through burning.

As I mentioned before that this is not a teaching against cremation but gives a good understanding of both Christian and Pagan burials. Your choice will influence the generations after. In my opinion cremation is not supported by the Bible....

Expense Comes With Cremation

Also there is expense that comes with cremation. You may want to avoid the $4,000 charge for cremation services. A traditional Christian burial can be done for literal pennies in comparison. For me a Christian burial is good conscience and savings at the same time.

Anyone can do this but team work is best....You may think that you will not be strong enough to do this but remember there are only a few simple steps...and it is amazing what we can accomplish when the pressure is on and when we work together with family.

Team work is best...

You can do this on your own however the old saying is true that two heads are better than one, and there is strength in numbers. Team work brings wisdom, confidence and strength. Have a friend or family member that will work closely with you. It is amazing the strength that comes as a team. You can go the distance to bless your loved one with a memorable funeral while guarding your family from the pressures and drain of major financial stress. It is amazing what you can face when you encourage each other. If you are alone you can follow the simple steps and achieve it too!! You also have a greater power that will help you through this difficult time. Father God is faithful to see you through so you are never alone.

Share your plans

You will need to share your plans for burial with the administrator of the nursing home or rehabilitation center and the case worker if your loved one has one. They are going to want to know what your plans are and that you are not planning to allow a funeral home to take care of things but you are planning to have a family burial.

Since I lived a distance from the nursing home where my father was staying, administration at the home required that my father be transported to a funeral home until I could get there to take care of things. Maybe there are some nursing homes that can provide refrigeration so going through a funeral home is not required. In my father's case they would not hold my father at the nursing home upon his passing so he had to be transferred to a funeral home.

Secrets Funeral Directors do not want you to know....

There is no law that says you have to go through a funeral home in the state of Maine. The funeral home is meant to present their services that will meet your family's needs. If you do choose to go through them understand that you are in charge. You should listen carefully to what they are sharing and do online research before you agree to any purchase. You can order products wholesale online or at a local businesses and do not have to be stuck with the high markups that come with relying solely on a funeral home. You will need to step back and ask yourself if you really need the items they suggest. Also does your loved on need it. They are with the Lord and would want you financially able to continue on with little pressure.

It is important to have a local funeral home in mind since there are is a free form that you will need from them. The form can be obtained from your local town office but many times you will be directed to a funeral home to obtain the form. The forms you will need are mentioned later in the book. If your loved one passes on a weekend you will have to keep them refrigerated until the town office opens on Monday in order to file the needed forms to transport the body to the cemetery. You may not be able to bypass the funeral home altogether.

When I say that you do not have to go through a funeral home, please understand legally that it is a fact, however since the town office seldom has family burials and nursing homes seldom hear of them, they are not sure of the laws that apply and automatically refer you to funeral homes. My father passed in the afternoon on a Monday so we were able to have him transferred to a funeral home in his home town until we were able to travel the following day and tend to the needed paper work and other final details.

Understand that if you have to go through a funeral home look for the cheapest way through it. I had my father held only a few hours there and was able to legally remove him quickly and take care of all major costs on my own. Just to have him held there for such a brief time I was charged over $600.00. Be very careful of seeds of doubt that funeral directors try to plant and understand that with these few simple steps you can save thousands. I did and you can too. Understand that most of what they will try to sell you, you do not need to buy into. I did not communicate my plans with them, only the legal side of things. I mentioned the forms needed and let them know I was aware of the procedures I had to take for a family burial. That kept them quiet as they observed my determination to achieve my goal.

They knew they would not be able to sell me their bill of goods, so they didn't.

*Laws vary from state to state. In Maine remember that there are no laws that require you to go through a funeral home...This **will save you thousands of dollars** since there is a fee for just about every service they offer.*

There is no law that requires your loved one to be embalmed...

You can save up to $500.00 dollars if you do not have your loved one embalmed.

However if you are not going to have your loved one embalmed then it is Maine state law that requires your family member to be buried within 24 hours from the time of death. We chose not to embalm my father and had a closed casket committal. However you are welcome to have a viewing for your family member and to apply make up if you wish but they must be buried within a twenty-four hour period.

Free Burial Plots

Purchasing a burial plot can cost hundreds or a few thousand dollars. Some rural cemeteries in Maine provide <u>free burial plots.</u> In some small towns if a person lives there for a year or more they are entitled to a free burial plot so my father received his for free having lived in the area for years. Just call the local town office and ask to speak with the cemetery caretaker then ask them if they offer burial plots free of charge. My father qualified and that was a huge savings.

Free Head Stone

Dad completed four years with the U.S. Air Force and qualified for a free head stone. In order to receive the head stone I had to wait until my father's passing then go online to www.va.gov and fill out VA Form 1330. I then had to provide his social security or service number found on his DD-214 then fill in the form and send it in. The free head stone was a great savings since the lowest price starts at $300.00 and goes higher. My father's free memorial stone values at $800 or more. The cemetery caretaker offered to set the stone however my husband and I plan to set it.

An article in a local paper stated that grave markers are provided free in most cemeteries here in Maine. A grave marker provides the name of the individual, date of birth and date of death. You will need to check with the cemetery caretaker to see if one will be provided for your loved one if they should need it.

Burial Vaults and Grave Liners

The State of Maine has no law that burial vaults or grave liners are mandatory.

Though some cemeteries do require that you have them most rural ones do not. It is important to ask the care taker of the cemetery if they require you to use a vault or if you can bury your loved one without a vault. If they require you to purchase a vault or liner then you have the option to check other cemeteries and find one that does not require them.

The cost is about the same as the casket. However the liners are a little cheaper.

Fortunately the cemetery caretaker said we did not need a cement vault or liner. (A vault is a container that would hold the casket. The vault is supposed to keep the ground level so it does not cave in over time.)

I have learned that the price of vaults range from around $1,500.00 and higher. It would have been double the price since my father was a big man.

Instead of going to a funeral home to price a vault I decided to go directly to the source. I called a cement company since they make the vaults. The sales person asked me if I was a funeral director. I told her no. She said that she could not sell to me since if the funeral directors found out that they sold a vault to me the funeral homes would no longer do business with the company. She said I was doing what they didn't want. She told me that her price was $700. So you can imagine the mark up a funeral home would put on one. The fact is that mark ups on vaults that a funeral home provides is big. All you have to do is Google and see the many services they provide at ridiculous prices. And most are unnecessary. Funeral homes understand that many people are desperate and vulnerable at that time and do not wish to think of their loved ones passing. They know that people do not do the research to find out that they do have options to bring about great financial savings and blessings to their family. So the family is at the mercy of the funeral home and their outrageous mark ups. People tend to wait until a loved one passes to find that a funeral home is about the only option they have since they waited to long to learn that they had other options that would save money big time.

I found this web site link where you can save up to 75% on vaults if you should need one.

Casket & Monument Discount
http://casketdiscount.com/vantage%20vault.htht

It may cost a little to have it delivered but no where near the mark up that it would be if you purchased it through a funeral home.

Cheapest Caskets Around

I have learned that there is no law or requirement in the State of Maine that says that you must buy your casket through a funeral home...

That is huge since they mark them up sometimes two to three hundred percent or greater.

Ask your family for financial help

Don't go it alone since even $100.00 can be a big help! I needed the best deal on a casket I could find. My brother offered to pay for it. He was close financially. I found a few great deals on the internet but felt I needed to find something local that would not include shipping charges. I found the cheapest route, e-mailed the information and we both agreed to contact the company. Then the final arrangements were made and we secured the casket at a very low cost. Since my brother lives in New York and I live in Maine the internet was a wonderful way for us to expedite things along.

Purchase the casket in State

You can avoid freight charges and delivery fees if you do and it also makes transfer to the cemetery simple when your loved ones passing occurs. You can opt to pick up the casket yourself and avoid the $100.00 delivery feel if you purchase the item local.

You need to call the Cemetery Director

The cemetery caretaker said that we would need a pine box casket or stronger wood, so we chose poplar since it is stronger than pine. My father weighed 400 pounds so we needed a very sturdy wood.

Purchasing the casket is one of the big expenses....

The casket is one of the big expenses to consider when planning your loved ones burial. Dad mentioned time and again that he wanted something simple since he would be gone anyway and did not want to put the family into unnecessary debt. So the question you must ask and be at peace with is what would they want? A fancy casket that would put your family in debt or would they want something practical that serves the same purpose but will render huge savings for their loved ones? Most would want to save the family from being burdened financially since they understand that we are the ones that must continue living in this challenging world. With a dollar being harder to find today this is a reality that should be considered. The price for a coffin for an average size person is $3,000 and higher. My father was 400 lbs and 6 feet tall so the cost would have been double! The cost of a pine box on the other hand, that is the average 5 to 6 ft., 24 wide to 15 high is considerably less.

I spoke with my brother about the casket and he offered to pay for it. The total cost for the oversized poplar casket was $1,780.00, compared to $6,000 or more. Even if you have to pay for it yourself that is a terrific savings!!! If you are capable of making your own casket it can be as little as $100.00 to $200.00 dollars for materials alone and can be an even greater savings.

Because my father's was an oversized casket it took four weeks to have the casket built so you should figure in the time needed. Ordering it in advance can have it handy in the event a loved one should pass unexpectedly. Also you will want it unfinished since it will save you money if it is natural wood. You can always add varnish when it is completed. To be earth friendly you do not need to apply varnish.

We purchased padding and silk material to line the interior and staple gunned it in place. I also made a pretty pillow with lace lining.

Save Money on Delivery Fee
We saved the $100.00 delivery fee by picking the casket up ourselves at the company and brought

our own flat bed truck to pick it up. We roped it in and drove it home.

We also saved by putting the hardware on ourselves. It is amazing how much you can save by cutting cost on the basic additions that you can do yourself.

I knew my Father's casket had to be special made and that we simply did not have the money for it. I learned that even talking with a funeral director cost me so I avoided them and did my research on my own.

I had heard my mother in times past mention that she wanted to be buried in a pine box. To me that sounded a bit uncomfortable and crude. While searching for a casket on the internet I happened to see a web site listed under Maine Pine Box. I clicked on the site and was quite impressed with its fine quality and craftsman ship. After being sickened by the high priced caskets I saw online I was delighted and relieved to see a savings as great as $3,000 and more. I immediately contacted my brother and let him know about the site. He checked it out and said that he was able to pay for an unfinished pine casket and within hours the building began.

Notes To My Brother

The following is correspondence by e-mail as my brother and I made arrangements to have the casket built.

Hi Tony,
I found this site. The company is located here in

Maine. Mr. Jones makes Pine Box caskets. The price is cheaper than regular ones. You are welcome to check out the site. Also his note is included at the bottom. The unfinished type without the veneer added is considerably cheaper.

Love,

Laurie

Laurie,

Right now money is tight. If you want to pre-purchase the casket I can probably buy the unfinished casket now.

Tony

Hi Tony,

So sorry to hear of your financial situation. We are very close also. It would be a real help if you can go ahead and purchase the unfinished casket. That would be a great contribution to the funeral expenses. You are welcome to contact Mr. Jones at 207 776-2444

Thank you very much.

Love,
Laurie

Hi Laurie,

I think everything is together now.

An oversize custom coffin 6'4" Long X 42" Wide X 25" High, plain unfinished, metal handles hinges and latches.

Box cost - $1,600
Maine State Sales Tax - $80
Delivery to Bridgeton - $100

TOTAL $1,780
 One half Due at Start = $890
 The remainder ($890) due on delivery.

I'll try to call your brother and let him know. I had his email address, but lost that somehow. Could you give me his email in case I can't get him by phone?

Thanks.

Mr. Jones

Laurie,

It is started. I will pay the rest upon completion.
Tony

This was a huge savings to me and time was of the essence. I was delighted and agreed for him to go ahead with the purchase. For an oversized specially made coffin, I had yet to find a better price anywhere. Plus the company was close enough for us to pick up the casket our selves and also save Tony the $100.00 delivery fee.

Another letter to Tony

Hi Tony,

The city of Camden has given me the right to obtain a form for transfer of remains so the cost of a limo is not needed. With the vault issue taken care of things are pretty much in place.

I will only need a funeral home in the event Dad should pass over the weekend and his body should need to be kept in refrigeration until the first of the week when I can obtain the from to transfer. I am not sure of the cost of refrigeration and plan to call a Funeral Home in Ellsworth. A small grave marker is available online for $300.00 so I am thinking of purchasing it.

We are very happy to have gotten the major bases covered now. Thank you so much again. I plan to contact you when he passes and let you know when the service will take place. I will love to see you and I know Aunt Rose, Aunt Kay and the family will too.

Love,
Laurie

Hi Tony,

I am very happy to say that the cemetery is not requiring a vault or liner. That is a huge savings. They said that we need a pine box and I told them that it will be taken care of.

I made arrangements with a friend of the family that has a backhoe. He charges $80.00 an hour and does not think the job will take any time to do. He will be on call for us in the event of Dad's passing. The caretaker plans to mark the grave off this morning for him to know just where to dig.

The Digging Begins

We heard of my father's passing Sunday, November 23rd, 2009 in the mid afternoon. By law my father had to be buried within 24 hours since he would not be embalmed. The trip we had to make was a four hour drive from our home. I had prearranged to have the grave site dug by having a friend of the family on and on call basis. We called him directly after receiving the news and he immediately got in touch with the Cemetery Director to look at the exact burial location. Our friend brought his backhoe to the designated site and the digging process began.

The following morning my husband went outside to place the casket that was in storage on our property back onto our flat bed truck. The nursing home contacted us and told us that

Dad was taken to the local funeral parlor to hold until we could get him. Time was of the essence now and we had to do everything quickly.

Nursing Home Requirements

The nursing home required my father to be transferred to a funeral home. Some nursing homes may not require this. If you live in the area that your loved one passed away in you may be able to bypass the funeral home altogether. You will need to have the steps in place in order to do so.

We lived three hours away and my father passed in the early afternoon on Sunday. He was immediately transferred to the local funeral home and was in refrigeration until we could get to him in the morning. The cost for transfer and refrigeration was $648.00. and an additional cost for each night would have been applied. Fortunately we needed their services for only one night.

Copy of Death Certificate

After hearing of my father's passing we awoke early Monday morning and took the four hour journey to the town where my father's physician was located. He was the last assisting physician present at time of death. He would be the one signing the Death Certificate. Normally a funeral home picks up the signed Death Certificate from the last assisting physician. In this case I learned that I as able to do so being next of kin. The doctor stalled us and finally learned that we were able to pick it up and so we did.

I had to have a copy of the death certificate in order transfer the remains of my father to the cemetery. Since Dad was held at the funeral home for a short time the doctor was able to communicate with them. They both understood that I indeed had the right to the certificate and so he released it to me.

Permit of Disposition Form

We then drove back to the Ellsworth where my father was held in storage. I had to request a transfer of remains form from the funeral home. You can pick the form up at any town office but they prefer you to go through a funeral home so I did. The funeral director was helpful. He helped me understand the need to fill in every blank on the transfer of remains form otherwise it would not be accepted. He said to be sure to put N/A in the fields that did not apply. If I did not the town would not accept the form and time was of the essence.

Forms Filed

Death Certificate and Permit of Disposition Forms Filed at the Town Office.

It was required to have the Death Certificate in hand along with the filled out Permit of Disposition Form when at the town office in order to request to transfer the remains of my father to the cemetery. Once approved by a Municipal Officer at the town office I then had to bring a certified copy of the approved Permit of Disposition back to the funeral director.

I was told by the funeral home director that the town office would most likely not approve the forms to transfer my father's body and that we may very well be denied. He mentioned that if that was the case then we would have had to take the matter to the Vital Statistics Department in Augusta. That could have taken days to get permission and would have meant extra money for holding Dad at the funeral home. However we were approved by the town without question and were in and out of the office in less than five minutes.

We paid the funeral director $645.00 in full. The director smiled and said that yes, we saved thousands by doing a family burial. Our biggest problem in dealing with all of this was getting past the concerns that the funeral director presented about the two necessary forms that needed to approved and filed. I understood that I would face some resistance from funeral directors in this area before hand and I did. You may too but it is only two forms that will save you thousands of dollars when signed and filed.

The final step after burying my father was to mail in a copy of the Permit of Disposition to the town office that my father was buried in so that they would be aware that he was placed there.

So basically the only two forms needed was the Death Certificate and The Permit of Disposition. This may be different in other towns. There may be more forms involved so it is important to check with your town office concerning family burial.

Save on Limo Expense

The director had the casket removed from our flatbed truck and he and two other large men transferred my father's body into the casket then lifted the casket back on our truck and we were on our way to the cemetery. I could have spent hundreds of dollars to transfer my father by using a limousine service but chose to save money doing it myself.

A Backhoe Is The Solution

We had one final obstacle to jump over. We had arrived at the grave site. It was a damp cold, rainy evening and the sun had not quite set. We were told that we would have some of the local people to help lower Dad's casket down into the grave. It weighed close to six-hundred pounds and we would need at least four strong men. We had called previously and the person that was supposed to help us was not in. My husband suggested that we call the person that dug the grave with his backhoe to and see if he would be able to lower the casket from the truck into the grave. He agreed and was at the burial site within minutes. He, his son and my husband tied ropes to the coffin and then to the back hoe and guided it smoothly down in. Then dirt was placed on top and the final job was done. We then had a small committal service. The backhoe is truly the way to go if you are short handed. The total cost for our friend to do the job was $120.00.

I placed a few sentimental items on his grave site. We plan to inform the family of a grave side ceremony that is to be held in the Spring when family is home from Florida.

My aunt Rose and my brother Tony informed me of the veteran's benefits and free burial stone. Upon my fathers passing I sent in for his free grave stone and have since received it from the Veteran's Administration of Maine. It weighs over 200 pounds and is beautiful. The cemetery caretaker offered to set the stone but we told him we would take care of the setting in June.

My father grew up in the area and many of his family are buried in the same cemetery so he has gotten his final wishes. We have too. Knowing he was well taken care of by those that loved him. And we are blessed with no financial strain. I enjoyed having my father in our truck on the way to the cemetery. I felt close to him there and felt this would be something he would have wanted. We loved our many rides together over the years and I knew it was our final ride together until eternity.

A Final Note To Family

Dear Family,

I don't mean to bring things back to finances but when we are all close, savings in such a situation as this matters. I could only see a title wave of expense headed our way...God is good to help and guide. These are just a few miracles in all of this. I had been seriously desiring and talking to the Lord about Dad's condition and the ground freeze that is taking place here. If he had lived much longer we would have had to put him in storage and that could have been a very expensive winter having to wait till Spring for burial. God is good to have spared us. He only had to be transferred and kept at the funeral home until I arrived and processed the release forms necessary to transfer him to the cemetery legally. I understand that closer is important and viewing Dad may have been a blessing for some but we would have had to have him embalmed and that would have been an added $400 to $500 dollars. As it was we paid the funeral home $649.00 just to have him transferred and held in refrigeration till we got there. Tony helped by paying for the casket a total cost of $1,780.00 so we were so blessed for his kind donation and support. $125.00 for backhoe including burial. There was no fee to file and receive the needed papers for transfer. The total cost was $2,744.00. Considering the average funeral is $7,000 or more just for an average size man, Dad's would have been double.

The funeral director said that for family to handle these matters is very rare and then he went on to say that he thought the town would disapprove the transfer forms but learned different since they were approved. The town could have insisted not to cooperate and the matter would have had to have been taken to Augusta and that would have taken at least another two days or more to get things taken care of. That would have been more money to keep Dad in refrigeration too. God is good to help things go smoothly.

Funerals are never easy and the strength to do this has been with much help from God. In my most trying moments a friend "happened" to be at the cemetery sitting in her car and invited me to chat with her as the casket was being lowered in the ground. She had similar stories of her own that let me know she understood and I knew the Lord was there with his comfort at such a needed time.

After the burial we went to the nursing home and

Ralph went in to pick up Dad's things as I waited in the truck. Linda, Dad's social worker "happened" to be at the front door of the nursing home when we arrived at 4:30 PM. And assisted us to quickly get his remaining things. God has given strength, peace, comfort and favor at every turn and now it is accomplished. All glory to Him alone. Ralph has been a great strength and encouragement through prayer, support, wisdom and action when needed during this time.

We feel It is only proper to wait until family is in the area to give everyone a chance to honor Dad's life, so upon Aunt Rose's request we plan to wait until early Spring or summer and then hold a grave side service. You will be informed as to just when this will take place.

Much love and peace in Father God's goodness. He will carry you and heal every area of your heart with time.

Love,

Sister

Steps in review

Please note that the high priced items that you want to get at wholesale prices are the casket, cement vault, burial plot, head stone, transporting your loved one.

1. When talking with the nursing home or funeral director you need to take charge and make it clear that you are planning to hold a family funeral by

going through the funeral home for the Form of Disposition only or as little as possible. Their job is to make money. Lots of money. Yours is to save, save, save. If they resist go to the Town Office and request the form there. Have all of this in place well before there is a need.

2. No need to pay for burial insurance if you have a good family burial in place.

3. Make preparations before your loved one passes.

4. Work together by contacting family and friends via emails or letters telling them of your financial situation. Encourage them to help you with emotional support and to work with you financially in order to achieve your goals.

5. See if you can obtain a free burial plot from family or the town for free or at a reduced price. You will need to call your town office and communicate with the cemetery caretaker.

You can also bury your family on your own property with permission and from your local Town Office.

6. Go online and price the cheapest caskets available. Try to do this well in advance of your loved ones passing. Find a local company. Google Pine Box Caskets. You may need to look online in surrounding states to find a casket company. Once purchased be sure to pick it up yourself in order to save the delivery fee. Encourage family to chip in for the expense. E-mail to them the web site and item of interest and you may be surprised to find a family member that will be willing to pay the entire cost. It happened for me and I am forever

grateful to my brother for his kind and generous support. Remember the casket is a major part of the expense. I have found that Pine Box Coffins are the cheapest way to go. (If you want to go green purchase an unfinished one. Great for the environment since it is all natural wood with no harmful varnish.)

7. Find a cemetery that does not require cement vaults or linings. These can cost as much as the coffin. If you must get one, go directly to the source. Google companies that make vaults in your state or in a neighboring state and talk with them directly. Tell them your need and if they will sell it to you at the lowest price. Remember in most states it is not a legal requirement to have a vault or liner. If the cemetery requires them you can obtain a note to counter their request.

8. Know that it is not law to embalm. You will save $400 to 500.00 dollars if you do not and it is another environmentally friendly process to avoid.

9. Before the death of your loved one, call the person with the backhoe and have them know where the site is and just when they should begin digging the grave.

10. Have family or friends to help lift the casket on to a flatbed truck and secure with ropes.

11. Obtain the signed Death Certificate from the last doctor that assisted your family member. Usually it is your loved ones family doctor.

12. Drive to the same town that the loved one passed away in and obtain a Permit of Disposition Form from your town office or funeral home there.

13. Get copies made of the Death Certificate since you may need it for other business matters after the burial is over. Such as dealing with bank accounts your family member may hold and finalizing bills that they may be coming to you.

With the signed Death Certificate and filled out Permit of Disposition Form in hand go to the town office in the same town of death and have a Municipal Officer approve and file the two documents with the town. Have a certified copy of the Permit of Disposition made to give to the funeral home. He in turn should give you a copy to file with the town where your loved one will be buried. After the burial you will need to simply mail it to the town office where your loved one is laid to rest. (If you did not go through a funeral home then be sure to mail a certified copy of the Permit of Disposition to the town office where your loved is buried.)

14. Remember that if you do not have your loved one embalmed according to Maine State law you have 24 hours from the time of death to perform the burial. I spoke with the local funeral home about my desire to have a family burial. I let them know that I understood that it was not state law for me to go through them and that I only wanted minimal services. I let them know I would need their services to transfer my father from the nursing home to the funeral home since the hospital would not hold his body and also I wanted to know the cost of keeping him at the funeral home in refrigeration for each night and until the fist day of the week in the event he should pass during the weekend. I refused any extra perks but agreed to only basic needs since each service offered was a few hundred extra.

15. Transport the body to the cemetery. We did this in our flat bed truck. The funeral home had a few strong men to lift my father who was in the casket into the truck. Be sure to have the lid sealed shut well with a few nails. With a copy of the Permit of Disposition in hand we then traveled 45 minutes to the grave site.

16. The grave site was dug. You should have a back hoe ready at the site to lift the casket off the truck and lower it into the burial plot. If you have friends and family to do the lifting then that is fine. However if not a back hoe will do the job well and quickly. For heavy family members it does the job well. Make sure there are plenty of heavy ropes available to fully tie on to the casket in order for the back hoe to get a secure grip.

17. We had a closed casket in order to bury my father quickly so as to abide by the 24 hour law.

18. Go home and heal for a while. Then send invitations for an inexpensive grave side memorial service. It brings family and the community near to your loved one. It also saves the expense of renting a hall. Have family make refreshments and meet at a family members home after the memorial service is over or at a park or beach area.

My prayer is that you will be blessed greatly by these steps. I truly have been.

Final Total Cost

My Brother Tony spent $1,780.00 for the pine box casket from a local company.

$40.00 round trip for gas to pick up casket.

$150.00 gas round trip for flatbed truck to transport the casket eight hours to the nursing home, funeral home and burial site.

$649 to have my father transferred to the funeral home and kept for one night in refrigeration.

$125.00 dollars for two hours of backhoe use.

Expense for lifters and pole bearers was $0.

Grave Stone was free through the Veterans Administration.

The plot was free from the town since my Dad lived there for over a year.

No Vault or liner was required. $0

No Limousine costs. $0

My total cost was $964.00 paid in full.

Total cost: $2,744.00

Considering my father was the size of two men and costs for a casket alone could have run as much as $10,000 or more not including all the other services. We saved an amazing amount of money. You will too. My advice is to plan ahead. You are well able to do this even with short notice. We did and you can too.

Almost a year has passed since I first published this book. I have had to wait until family returned from wintering in Florida in order to hold my father's memorial service.

I recently submitted his obituary in his home town local paper and will travel there soon to be with family. The fascinating thing is that the news paper editor would not publish his obituary announcement with out first me giving the name of the funeral home that had taken care of my father for that brief time. It shows just how times have changed and how truly dependent we have become on funeral homes and just how much they are taking advantage of the public with their high mark ups.

I have come to understand that most of our expense that can bankrupt a family is end of life expenses because of extended stays in hospitals and then burial cost. Imagine a family that incurs such cost as they care for multiple family members.

The obituary I had written and submitted via e-mail was only an additional $85.50 with his photo included.

After the memorial service I am not holding a meal or snack time in a hall. We are meeting at my father's favorite park near the ocean. Free of charge.

I have sent invitations that I created on Publisher and included in the invitation that all are welcome to bring something sweet if they wish for after the service. You may think this is a little to chinsey but you can only spend what you have. Many blessings as you consider and possibly utilize the information in this brief book.

Final Thoughts and Memories

My husband and I were recalling Dad's jovial laughter today. It was as if we could see him so clearly in our mind!!! He truly left an imprint of love and good will with many people. Warm memories are kept in my heart from my youth of watermelon in the park, cotton candy at the many fairs and zoos, quite times at the lake fishing and long rides in the country are now a thing of the past but will remain forever. I am very thankful for the many joys that my Father gifted the family with of good times and laughter.

The most wonderful gift was that of our faith in God. He loved the Lord and wrote many songs that would lift Jesus up. That is a legacy that is without price.

I wrote this poem for my Father just after his passing.

Midnight Train

Midnight train of darkness bright
I helped you board for your last ride.
The final gray evening shadows loom,

I see the grim gleam of hope and healing in your eyes.

Oh sweet release that lies beyond,

The tall pale conductor beckons, aalllll aboard!!!

Gray and chilly, swirling winds,

Bittersweet the engine sings...

Healing, hope, healing hope, healing, hope...as the train chugs into eternity.

Oh midnight train of darkness bright, comes for someone every second!!!

All too soon you'll hear the sound, ready or not here I come!!!

Don't sit at the station and wait and wait,

Set goals and make a difference till your very last breath!!

Say your I love yous, be quick to forgive!!!

And be sure your heart is right with the Lord.

Oh midnight train.

Laurie Knight

www.ingramcontent.com/pod-product-compliance
Lightning Source LLC
Chambersburg PA
CBHW062103280526

45788CB00003B/1333